Original title:
The Purpose of Life: Does It Have One?

Copyright © 2025 Creative Arts Management OÜ
All rights reserved.

Author: Amelia Montgomery
ISBN HARDBACK: 978-1-80566-152-8
ISBN PAPERBACK: 978-1-80566-447-5

Fleeting Glimpses of Truth

In the quest for a silver spoon,
We trip over shoelaces, oh what a tune!
Searching for answers in a cereal box,
While squirrels plot our demise like sly foxes.

Life's a circus full of clowns,
Juggling dreams, turning frowns upside down.
Maybe we're just here for the cake,
Or to learn silly moves in life's wobbly wake.

Navigating the Stars Above

Stargazing with waffles on a plate,
Does Mars have a café? Let's not hesitate!
The Milky Way's looking quite crispy tonight,
While aliens laugh at our earthly plight.

Constellations keep changing their clothes,
Perhaps stardust is just glitter from those?
Astrology says I should go for a jog,
But I think I'll just snuggle my lazy dog.

A Symphony of Questions

Why do socks vanish into thin air?
Are they plotting a world without a care?
Does the moon get lonely shining alone?
And why can't my plants just answer my phone?

Each question a noodle in a soup of thought,
Like puzzles that leave us twirling and caught.
Do fish ever wonder about our dry land?
Or do they just think we're terribly bland?

Shadows Speak in Colors

Shadows dance when the sun's feeling cheeky,
Painting rainbows while calling life freaky.
If laughter's the answer, why's my punchline flat?
Are we just the jesters in some cosmic chat?

Colors whisper secrets in a drunken spree,
As I sip lemonade beneath the old tree.
Perhaps we're just actors in a goofy play,
With stage props of dreams that sometimes go stray.

The Colors of Curiosity

With a brush in hand, I paint each day,
But oh dear friend, where's the buffet?
Mixing hues of laughter, a splash of cheer,
Searching for answers, yet they disappear.

Tickle the fancies, ride a wild horse,
Who knew a cow could change your course?
Life's a jigsaw, pieces all askew,
But I still suspect there's magic in glue.

Canvas of the Heart

On my canvas, I paint with glee,
A rainbow unicorn named Mr. McGee.
His glittery mane shines bright in the sun,
Yet still, I ponder, are we just for fun?

I dabble in colors, each shade a dream,
Mixing yellow socks with raspberry cream.
Life's an odd canvas, a quirky art show,
And now I'm out of paint—where'd it go?

Symphony of Solitude

In a symphony of quirks and frantic beats,
I dance alone to my own two left feet.
The music echoes, oh what a ball,
Was that a note or my phone's awful call?

A maestro of mischief, I twirl in delight,
Chicken dance, electric slide, oh what a sight!
Life's a concert where we often forget,
To bring an umbrella—oh, what a wet set!

Whispers in the Wind

The wind whispered secrets, a silent jest,
While I chased it down in a polka dot vest.
It laughed in my face, oh what a tease,
Was that wisdom or just a sneeze?

I huffed and I puffed, I followed the breeze,
Past dancing squirrels and trees with no leaves.
Life's but a riddle wrapped in a grin,
So let's tune in with laughter—where do we begin?

Fleeting Moments

In the morning, I spill my tea,
Wondering if that's meant to be.
A bird laughs, drops some bread,
Is this how we move ahead?

Time dances on the kitchen floor,
Chasing socks, it's never bored.
I trip on life, I fall with glee,
Is this what it's supposed to be?

My dog barks at a passing car,
"Is that the meaning?" - not so far.
I throw him treats, we laugh and play,
Is this how we spend our day?

Lasting Thoughts

I ponder deep in the shower's mist,
Why socks always end up like this.
The echoes giggle, the soap does slide,
Is wisdom hiding where I abide?

Under piles of laundry, I seek truth,
Was it lost at age—let's say, youth?
My cat ponders life with a skeptical glance,
Is it all just a maddening dance?

I write down dreams with a pencil stub,
Always forgetting where I was, oh, drub!
The ink flows wildly, like thoughts reeling,
Life's a circus, or is it just feeling?

The Silence Between Breath

Inhale, exhale, do I exist?
The fridge hums tunes that can't be missed.
A toast to silence, a whisper here,
Does the sandwich know why I cheer?

With every breath, I contemplate,
Why do I talk to forks on this plate?
Do they judge me as I try to dine,
Or just sit there, wondering at the wine?

My dog snorts, dreams of chasing cats,
Is his life better? All those naps and chats?
Yet, when he barks, I wonder anew,
Is he asking the same questions too?

Artistry of Intent

I paint my nails a vivid hue,
Swearing it's art, that much is true.
With every stroke, is there a sign?
Or just a mess of colors divine?

I sculpt my lunch into a grand feast,
It's pizza art, not just a beast!
Each slice a canvas, it makes me grin,
Is culinary a win-win?

A sneeze erupts—oops, there's my spice!
Did creativity take my advice?
With tomato splatters, I can't complain,
This mess is surely art, with no restrain!

Mirages of Meaning

On the horizon, I spy a clue,
Is it a mirage, or something true?
With every step, my thoughts unwind,
Is clarity just a frame of mind?

Fuzzy clouds pass up in the sky,
Each looks like something, oh my, oh my!
A castle, a monster, or just plain gray,
Are we all just shapes in the life display?

The ice cream melts as I ponder this,
Each drip a question I can't dismiss.
With each cone conquered, I smile and sigh,
Maybe the answers are just a pie!

Footprints on Celestial Paths

In space we float on words so light,
Hoping to catch a star tonight.
Aliens laugh at our silly quests,
While we search the sky like cosmic pests.

With pizza slices as our guide,
We roam the void, full of pride.
Each comet's tail a fleeting clue,
That maybe cheese is our dream too.

Mars is red, but we wear plaid,
Navigating like we're slightly mad.
Life's a joke, or so they say,
Why not laugh and dance away?

So if you stumble on a star,
Just remember laughter travels far.
Life's a giggle, hold it tight,
Through cosmic chaos, we ignite!

Tides of Reflection

The ocean waves whisper secrets bright,
While seagulls squawk, 'What a silly sight!'
We search for meaning in sandy shores,
Only to find a crab and some boars.

Is life just a loop like tide's retreat?
Or more like a fish with stinky feet?
We ponder depth in shallow pools,
As dolphins giggle – what are fools?

With every wave, a chance to play,
As seaweed dances in a spray.
The sandcastles crumble, oh what a mess,
Yet we laugh, because who needs success?

A beach ball life, full of cheer,
With sunscreen slathered from ear to ear.
Let's dive into the foam and splash,
For laughter's the treasure that we must stash!

Notes from the Abyss

In darkness deep, where shadows dwell,
I ponder if I smell a shell.
With squids reciting Shakespeare's lines,
And jellyfish wearing funny signs.

"Is this it?" asks an octopus,
While waving arms in grandiose fuss.
The current pulls, like a wild dance,
As starfish plead for just one chance.

In the abyss, a snail holds court,
Debating if life's a good sport.
With laughter echoing off cold stone,
Who needs a throne when you have foam?

So let's embrace the ocean's jest,
With sea cucumbers, we feel blessed.
Life's a soiree in waters deep,
Just don't forget your swimming sheep!

Radiance of the Unknown

In the realm of dreams where creatures glow,
I met a cat who said hello.
With stars for whiskers, it danced around,
Chasing shadows that made no sound.

We debated wisdom, oh what a laugh,
Is life a photo or just a gaffe?
With cosmic brownies and milk from the stardust,
We ponder existence, or was it just lust?

Galaxies twinkle, a subtle tease,
While we juggle planets with utmost ease.
Over here, a worm offers tea,
"Do you think life is just 'whoopee'?"

Let's take a spin on this wacky ride,
With comets flashing, like joy we can't hide.
Embrace the quirks, let laughter beam,
And dance through the unknown, like a vivid dream!

Echoes of Forgotten Dreams

In a world where socks disappear,
I ponder what I'm doing here.
A mug of coffee, a loaf of bread,
Or is that just what the baker said?

Do we chase butterflies or find a cat?
Is life a game of hide and spat?
Searching for wisdom in a bowl of stew,
Only to find it's not meant for you!

The distant echo of childhood glee,
Chasing clouds and climbing trees.
Yet here I stand, my dreams all jumbled,
Wondering why my toast is crumbled!

So here's to the wanderers and the lost,
Who laugh at the lines and the heavy cost.
We skip and trip on this winding path,
Finding joy in the unpredictable math.

The Dance of Serendipity

Two left feet on a dancing floor,
I twirl and trip, but what's in store?
Life's cue ball rolls, a surprise in sight,
I'll waltz through the chaos, oh what a fright!

With each misstep, I giggle and cheer,
Can't find my rhythm but never my fear.
Stumbling through puddles, I splash and grin,
Finding joy in the mess that lies within.

A dance with fate in a mismatched shoe,
I pirouette past the weeds that grew.
In the beat of the moment, I sway and spin,
Laughing at life and where it's been.

So grab a partner, let's take a chance,
In the awkwardness, there's always romance.
With a hop, skip, and a well-timed laugh,
We'll find our way on this quirky path.

Shadows of Intent in the Light

In the shadow of dreams, I peer and squint,
What's the motive? What's the hint?
A shadowy figure, playing coy,
Dancing around my scattered joy!

Am I a knight or a jester in disguise?
With rubber chicken and grandiose lies?
Searching for meaning in Netflix shows,
While the cat plots world domination, I suppose.

The light flickers in the late-night glow,
What's real and what's just a show?
Are we players on life's comical stage?
Or just scripts lost in a messy page?

I'll laugh in the shadows, dance in the light,
With each quirky whim and silly delight.
Embrace the absurd, let go of the fight,
For even in chaos, there's always a bite!

A Tapestry of Unanswered Questions

In a tapestry woven with threads of doubt,
I stitch together what life's about.
Is it yarn or string? Or something more grand?
A pattern of chaos, not quite planned.

What's laughter without a punchline, sweet?
A puzzle unsolved at life's quick retreat.
Chasing shadows with pockets of air,
Wondering if nobody truly cares.

Knitting together the fun and the frown,
Is purpose just wearing a goofy crown?
Life's an odd quilt, with patches so bright,
Sewn by the stitches of day and night.

So let's raise a glass to the questions we share,
In the midst of the quirk, we find we all care.
For in our confusion, we find our way through,
With laughter and love, in a patchwork we grew.

The Dance of Uncertainty

In a world where socks do stray,
We dance around, come what may.
With mismatched shoes and silly hats,
Who knows where life's adventure's at?

We juggle dreams with jelly beans,
And flip a coin for in-betweens.
When plans all flop like pancake bats,
We laugh and dance, imagine that!

A twist, a turn, we lose our way,
Directions lost, oh what a play!
Life's like a game of hopscotch feet,
Jumping through joy, oh what a treat!

So here's to life, both wild and neat,
With upside-down and offbeat beat.
To wiggle through each silly strife,
And have a giggle at this life!

Embraced by the Unknown

I packed my bags with a rubber duck,
Setting sails with a bit of luck.
On waves of doubt, I twist and twirl,
In search of treasure, give it a whirl!

Maps are scribbles, paths unclear,
But I embrace the quirk with cheer.
With half a compass and a snack,
I dance along this winding track!

Behind each bush, a mystery grows,
Is that a rabbit or just my toes?
Exploration's got me in a spin,
What's out there? Let's just dive in!

So here I go, a curious fool,
With laughter as my trusty tool.
In the unknown, I find my groove,
Life's a dance, and I just move!

Whimsical Paths of Discovery

If life were a pie, I'd take the slice,
Filled with giggles and topped with spice.
With forks that point in random spots,
I hop along the jumbled knots!

Every corner hides a crazy sight,
A dancing cat, a kite in flight.
I chase the whimsy, lose my way,
But stumble on a funny play!

Like rain on sunny picnic dreams,
Life's oddities are bursting seams.
I've found new friends in absurd places,
Like tangerines in silly faces!

So let's toast to the nonsensical fun,
Where every moment's a quirky pun.
In paths unknown, together we roam,
And make this wacky world our home!

Echoes of a Life Well-Lived

A honk, a woof, a squeaky toy,
Echoes of laughter, life's simple joy.
With high-fives from the gnomes in my yard,
I dance with shadows, swinging hard!

Each stumble's a step in the grand ballet,
Cartwheeling through the ups and downs of the day.
I trip on dreams and leap with glee,
Life's a circus — come join me!

With every snack break, wisdom grows,
Like marshmallows topped on a s'mores pose.
Embrace the quirks, the offbeat calls,
And waltz through life's wacky halls!

So here's to the echoes, the joyful rounds,
The silly moments that life surrounds.
In laughter's arms, I'll forever stay,
To echo right back, come what may!

Threads of Connection

We weave our tales with silly threads,
Each laugh a stitch, each sigh that spreads.
In coffee shops and parks we meet,
Trading jokes, our daily treat.

From wobbly bikes to awkward dances,
Life's a stage with funny glances.
In every quirk, a bond we find,
Connecting hearts and silly minds.

The hugest questions loom above,
But we just shrug and share our love.
With goofy hats and playful ways,
We chase the clouds through mundane days.

So let's embrace this wacky ride,
With laughter loud, we'll swing and slide.
For in our hearts, the truth's well-known,
In silly moments, we're never alone.

Transience and Time

Tick-tock goes the clock, oh dear!
Time's a prankster, bring us cheer!
We chase the minutes, what a race,
But all we get is more red face.

A fleeting glance, a fumble here,
We trip through life with giddy cheer.
The more we grasp, the less we hold,
In jest we find the truth so bold.

With every wrinkle, comes a tale,
Of mischief, giggles, never frail.
We live for moments that make us grin,
Through the maze of time, we laugh and spin.

So let's not fret or wear a frown,
For fleeting days will wear us down.
Embrace each spark, each goofy climb,
We're simply jesters, stopping time.

Ripples of Reflection

Mirror, mirror, on the wall,
Who's the silliest of them all?
Is it the one with the chicken hat?
Or perhaps it's me, who fell flat?

Life's a pool of jumbled thought,
With every dive, a lesson caught.
We splash and flail, what a sight,
In charm and chaos, there's delight.

Reflections stir when laughter's near,
We ponder deep while munching beer.
With every giggle, wisdom grows,
In randomness, truth lightly flows.

So here's to ripples, big and small,
To moments shared that conquer all.
In every jest, we find our way,
Through silly waters, come what may.

Mosaic of Moments

Life's a puzzle, don't you see?
With pieces scattered, wild and free.
Some fit quite well and some just flop,
But oh the fun, we'll never stop.

With laughter bits and giggly glues,
We stick together, share our views.
In colorful chaos, we find our ground,
In silly fortunes, joy is found.

So let's glue on those silly charms,
With unicorns and playful arms.
Each moment a tile, bright and bold,
In this mosaic, stories unfold.

And when it's framed, we'll step back,
With smiles so wide, oh what a knack!
For in this artwork, with all its hue,
The joy of life's the best view.

Whispers of Existence

In the morning light, I sip my tea,
Wondering what's next for a guy like me.
Is it just to eat cake and laugh out loud?
Or dance with my cat and feel quite proud?

Beneath the stars, I ask the night,
Do we just exist, or is that all right?
I tripped on a dream while chasing a beam,
But then I woke up, and it was a meme!

So, I scribble my thoughts on a napkin fair,
Hoping someone reads it, but who would care?
Perhaps I'll end up in a book someday,
Next to a recipe for a soufflé!

So here's to the laughs and joys we find,
Though questions abound, and they don't unwind.
We'll dance 'til dawn, not knowing the plan,
With ice cream in hand, life's just a big jam!

Threads of Meaning Unraveled

Strolling through life, I trip on a shoelace,
Searching for answers in this silly race.
Is it about fame or just having fun?
Or sneaking more snacks when no one's begun?

A squirrel once told me in a tree-top chat,
'Life's like a pancake; you flip it, you fat!'
So I got confused, but played along well,
A pancake, a squirrel—what more can I sell?

With friends in my corner and jokes up my sleeve,
I ponder the meaning, but can't quite believe.
If the road is a joke, I'll laugh as I roam,
Every twist and turn feels like coming back home!

So let's cheer and giggle throughout our days,
Finding delight in the strange, funny ways.
With ice cream and laughter, come take a ride,
Life's more fun filled with friends by your side!

A Quest Through Time's Labyrinth

Through twists and turns in a time-worn maze,
I chase after wisdom, lost in a haze.
What's the grand scheme? I just can't see!
Is it all for the joy of a good cup of tea?

Each corner I round brings a new kind of hair,
I meet past versions who can't help but stare.
'Do we have a map?' I shout with a grin,
'Or are we just wandering, hoping to win?'

With laughter as fuel and snacks in my pack,
I explore the unknown, never looking back.
Perhaps it's more fun if we just let it flow,
And make every wrong turn a new way to glow!

So here's to the journey, the curious quest,
May we find our own paths and give it our best.
In this wacky world, let's tickle some fate,
With giggles and snacks, isn't life just great?

Searching for Stars in a Cosmic Sea

In a cosmic boat, we sail through the night,
Hoping to catch stars that shimmer so bright.
Is existence a puzzle we're meant to solve?
Or just a grand game where we all evolve?

The moon winks at me, as if in on the joke,
'Life's just a riddle, now take a good poke!'
So I poke at my dreams and they giggle back,
While the universe chuckles, like a friendly quack.

I trade my fears for a handful of fun,
And dance with the comets, till daylight has won.
Are we just stardust enjoying our play?
Or cosmic comedians with quirks on display?

So let's chase the stars and float on a whim,
With laughter and laughter, our chances are slim.
But in this vast sea, we'll laugh till we drop,
For every good joke is a magical prop!

Canvas of Choices

Brush strokes of whimsy paint my days,
In colors of chaos, in puzzling ways.
I might be a giraffe, or an astronaut in disguise,
Each choice a wild giggle, under twinkling skies.

With each color splash, a new laugh I create,
Mixing reds with blues, inflating my fate.
A masterpiece forming, or just a big mess?
Yet in every mistake, I find joy, I confess.

Is my life an art show or a circus parade?
A juggler's fine dance? Or perhaps a charade?
With popcorn in hand, I just munch and I smile,
Embracing the chaos, it's all worth the while.

The Weight of Wonder

I ponder on mountains, the weight they may hold,
While sipping my coffee, feeling quite bold.
Are we here for the giggles or to toil like a bee?
My cat thinks it's snacks—what a life, can't you see?

So I ponder and wonder, lightweight and free,
Perhaps life's just a game of hide and seek glee.
With questions like balloons, floating high in the air,
I laugh at the riddles, no worry or care.

Why worry about journeys, when I've got pizza?
Life's a cheesy affair, yes sirree, let's tease ya!
Wrapped in my warmth, like a burrito delight,
With laughter and crumbs, I'll toast to the night.

Dancing with Uncertainty

Two left feet shuffling, I step in the fray,
For life's one big dance, it's a curious ballet.
Shall I spin to the left or do the cha-cha?
Who knew I'd mix salsa with singing in Mahabharata?

Each twist brings a chuckle, each turn brings a cheer,
In the dance of confusion, there's nothing to fear.
Do I jump in the air or just shuffle my socks?
With every wrong move, I invent new funny blocks.

So let's tango with riddles, and foxtrot with fate,
Life's a grand stage, don't be late, don't be late!
We'll waltz through the nonsense, with flair and delight,
Embracing each misstep, oh what a sight!

Beneath an Unbroken Sky

Underneath skies that refuse to crack,
I lie on my back, feeling no lack.
Are these clouds just fluff or have they got plans?
As they drift overhead, plotting out lands!

With every bright sunbeam, I bake like a pie,
Yet still I wonder, oh why, oh why?
Do squirrels know secrets, or is it all chatter?
While I ask these deep questions, my dreams seem to scatter.

Each star a comedian, each moonbeam a clown,
With my giggles and snacks, I'll never back down!
So I'll dance in the shadow of shadows and light,
Making fun of the mysteries that tickle the night.

Interludes of Introspection

Why am I here, at this fine brunch?
With eggs so fluffy, and toast to munch.
I ponder deep, with a fork in hand,
Is this what they meant by life so grand?

My cat looks wise, judging my fate,
While eyeing the fish that's on my plate.
Is purpose found in a purr or a snack?
Or buried deep down in a Netflix stack?

I chase my thoughts like a squirrel on a spree,
Do I exist for the coffee or finely baked brie?
Could it be laughter, shared over a meal?
Or just to ensure my socks never feel real?

With friends who giggle and spatula dreams,
We solve life's riddles over custard creams.
With smiles and puns united in cheer,
Is that the purpose? I think it's right here!

Silent Conversations with Eternity

I whisper sweet nothings to the empty air,
Debating with spirits who may or may not care.
Do I inquire meaning or roll up my sleeves?
Should I plant my roots or just dance with leaves?

Eternity chuckles from the vast unknown,
While I ponder hard over my cellphone.
With hashtags of wisdom and memes so profound,
Is truth in the laughter that echoes around?

As I scroll through regrets, life lessons, and gags,
I wonder if answers come tied in swag bags.
Should I meditate or just buy a new hat?
Are questions enough, or is that where I'm at?

In silent exchanges, the cosmos winks bright,
Do stars hold a purpose, or are they just light?
Perhaps the grand scheme is just pie for the soul,
Or really great jokes that make us feel whole!

Whims of the Heart

My heart's a jester, flipping its hat,
Saying 'let's dance,' while I'm chasing a cat.
Does love come wrapped in a funny old joke?
Or in the ice cream that makes me choke?

In whimsical days where sunshine's a must,
I ponder if living is missing the fuss.
Is joy in the chase or in the final score?
Or lurking behind that mysterious door?

With giggles and sighs, we wander the lane,
Questioning life while playing in the rain.
Could the secret be found in a sprightly jig?
Or in a flower-smelling, hilarious dig?

As laughter erupts like a soda pop stream,
I sense that existence is more like a dream.
In whimsical turns, may I find my part,
Could it be joy? Oh, the whims of the heart!

The Paradox of Living

I wake up each morn, with a smile and a yawn,
Trapped in a riddle since the day I was born.
Is life like a sandwich, just stacked up and neat?
Or a messy burrito, all wrapped in defeat?

I juggle my chores, like a caffeinated clown,
While contemplating if I should wear a crown.
Is life a grand circus, a show full of flair?
Or just a pie fight where nobody's aware?

With ups and with downs, it's a wild, silly ride,
It dances on fortune; it hides 'neath the tide.
Should I chase after meaning, or savor the fun?
Why choose just one path when there's always a pun?

Maybe the paradox is all in one breath,
Finding delight, even thinking of death.
As I laugh through the chaos and join in the fun,
I'll flip through the pages, till knowledge is done!

Dance of the Infinite

Life's a jig, a silly spree,
Twirl around, just wait and see.
Chasing dreams, it's a wild race,
Where's the finish? Just embrace!

Jumping high, we spill our juice,
Pizza slices, or maybe moose?
Laughter echoes in the air,
Is there more? Who knows? We dare!

Wobbling like a gummy bear,
Skipping here, and over there.
While we dance, time seems to fade,
Do we care? We've got it made!

Silly hats and mismatched shoes,
Facing fears, we laugh and choose.
In this mess, a truth we find,
Life's a giggle, love's unlined!

Voices of the Ancients

Once a sage with twinkly eyes,
Claimed he knew life's big surprise.
He scratched his head, he scratched his chin,
Turns out it's a game of win-win!

"Breathe deep, eat cake!" he said with glee,
"Or contemplate the flying bee!"
Before I could nod, he flew away,
Oh ancient dude, where'd you play?

With every whisper from the wise,
Comes a poke and funny prize.
Tales of yore and lots of jest,
Do you even know? It's a test!

Let's spin tales of grand delight,
In funny dances, day and night.
Voices rise in joyful sway,
What was the question? Hey, hooray!

The Melody of Mystery

Tickling keys on a rusty piano,
What's the song? Who's our great alto?
Sounds collide, a ruckus grows,
Mystery knocks, and in it goes!

Birds are singing, squirrels critiquing,
Notes at random, mischief peeking.
What does it mean? We laugh and jest,
In life's orchestra, we're all blessed!

Frogs croak rhythms, a silly beat,
They croon along, tapping their feet.
Dance with shadows, skip with the breeze,
Is it madness? Well, if you please!

Harmony in chaos lies,
Each note tells tales and silly highs.
In this tune, what have we found?
Life's a mystery, joy abound!

In the Realm of Possibility

Imagine worlds where tacos fly,
And kittens rule the sunny sky.
What can be? The mind can roam,
In every corner, there's a home!

Paint your dreams with colors bright,
In fluffy clouds, we take our flight.
The future's funny, oh what fun,
Grab your hat, and here we run!

Every twist, a chance to play,
In this realm, we'll find our way.
Juggling stars and chasing rays,
Today is ours, let's join the frays!

What if ducks wore shoes so fine?
Or painted bikes on grapevine?
The crazy things that life can share,
In the realm of fun, we laugh, we dare!

Threads and Tapestries of Thought

We weave with laughter, not a care,
Life's a pattern, we gladly share.
With silly strings and vibrant hues,
Creating tales of what we choose.

In tangled knots, we find our way,
A jumbled mess that seems to play.
Each absurd twist brings joy, not dread,
A patchwork quilt beneath our bed.

From silly socks to tangled hair,
It's all a dance, if you dare!
So grab your thread, let laughter flow,
In this crazy game, just go with the flow.

Life's a fabric, wild and bright,
Sewn with whims and pure delight.
If you trip on your own shoelace,
Just laugh it off, embrace the chase!

Light and Shadows of Hope

In shadows cast by pizza's glow,
We ponder why we're here, you know?
With extra cheese, our thoughts take flight,
In cheesy dreams, we seek the light.

The universe is vast, they say,
But here we sit and eat all day.
With every slice, a lesson learned,
Life's riddles tossed, and pizza burned.

A dance of crumbs and sparkling cheer,
We gather 'round, our hopes sincere.
With every laugh, we find our way,
And pizza crust, we do not sway.

So let's toast with our soda cups,
To life's great mystery, and all that ups.
With laughter bright, we'll take a chance,
In this crazy world, let's laugh and dance!

The Language of Seeking

We search for meaning, day and night,
With Google Maps and visions bright.
But when we glance at sushi rolls,
We find that joy fuels hungry souls.

In conferences of vacuum sales,
We stumble through with goofy tales.
Each question asked, a riddle spun,
In office chairs, life's a pun.

With every query, we may find,
A little laughter, quite unconfined.
In all the searches, big and small,
It's joy that answers best of all.

So grab a donut, take a bite,
In every moment, find your light.
For life's a question, fun and free,
In laughter's language, we can see!

Moments that Define Us

In a blink, we slip and fall,
Tripping over life's great hall.
With funny faces, we collide,
In awkward moments, joy can hide.

A missed cue in the dance of fate,
Turns simple steps to laughter's plate.
These blunders bright, they guide our way,
In mishaps found, we choose to play.

From chocolate stains to missed alarms,
We charm the world with silly charms.
Each moment slips, a fleeting grace,
In every trip, we find our place.

So here's to laughter, loud and clear,
In crazy times, we persevere.
Defining moments, let them land,
With open hearts, let's take a stand!

Beyond the Veil of Doubt

I ponder questions, oh so deep,
Like why my plants are all half-sleep.
I search for signs and flickering lights,
Is it all fate, or just my nights?

In dreams I ask the sky so wide,
Is my path carved or just a ride?
With tacos falling from above,
I laugh and question, what is love?

The squirrels advise from trees so tall,
They chat and chitter, yet it's all small.
Is life a joke, a cosmic jest?
Perhaps we're really in a test!

So here I stand, with snacks in hand,
Wondering if it's all just bland.
In capes we dance, let spirits prance,
For meaning's lurking in the chance!

A Journey Through Infinite Questions

I trotted forth on paths unclear,
With gummy bears to quell my fear.
Each turn I took, a laugh or two,
What's life but gumdrops, bright with hue?

The rivers flowed with fizzy drinks,
And thoughts would bounce like well-timed winks.
Do we exist for snacks and play?
Or is there more to this odd ballet?

A wise old cat, she sipped her tea,
Proclaimed life's just a big ol' spree.
With every giggle, doubts dissolve,
In silly moments, problems solve.

So I'll embrace this wobbly quest,
With jellybeans, I feel the best.
In every laugh, let joy expand,
And find delight in unplanned land!

Threads of Destiny

They say we're woven, thread by thread,
From silly socks to breakfast spread.
Is it all just a crazy quilt?
With tacos made from borrowed guilt?

In fabric stores, I seek my fate,
A patchwork heart that's never late.
With every stitch, I lost the plot,
Does this mean I'm simply what I bought?

With t-shirts sporting goofy quotes,
I question why the cow just gloats.
Life's a tapestry, bright and grand,
But why's there always mustard in my hand?

So let's embrace this wild design,
With mismatched socks that surely shine.
For in this chaos, we delight,
Threads of life weave laughs all night!

Echoes in the Silence

In quiet moments, whispers play,
Tickling thoughts in a goofy way.
I ponder matters vast and wide,
Yet giggle softly, what's inside?

The echoes bounce, they tease my brain,
Is it all just a poppy stain?
With every echo, I lose my track,
Flipping thoughts, they travel back.

A puddle forms, it splashes bright,
Reflecting doubts that shine with light.
Do we exist to sing and dance?
Or merely wander, lost in trance?

With every hush, a chuckle swells,
Life's simply baked like chocolate shells.
In echoes here, we glean the fun,
And dance with laughter, every one!

Through the Fabric of Time

In a world where socks roam free,
And Mondays laugh at you with glee,
We ponder over cosmic schemes,
While counting all our silly dreams.

The clock spins tales of missed trains,
While we're just chasing after gains,
But UFOs have better plans,
And all we've got are pizza stands.

Life's a riddle wrapped in a bike,
We ride with courage, take a hike,
But secretly we all just crave,
A nap beneath a sunny wave.

Yet here we are, a little lost,
At coffee shops, we laugh and toss,
Our worries like confetti fly,
Sipping dreams while time slips by.

Journeys in the Quiet

In the stillness, voices hum,
As squirrels plot with little drum,
We ask the stars, 'What's the deal?'
They wink at us and start to squeal.

Sipping tea with wise old trees,
While chaos dances in the breeze,
Our minds are busy, thoughts collide,
Like socks that flee the dryer wide.

In doodling dreams, we find a map,
To treasure chests and rabbit traps,
As we try to decode the night,
With giggles lost in borrowed light.

Oh, to wander without haste,
Mixing dreams with life's sweet paste,
Each moment a delight in kind,
As laughter echoes in our mind.

Chasing Fleeting Shadows

When shadows play their little games,
They jump around and change their names,
We chase them down and fall in ditches,
While questioning our riches and glitches.

Lifting umbrellas on sunny days,
We marvel at the moon's ballet,
But what is life if not a jest?
With every tick, we do our best.

We trip on dreams, not on the ground,
In a world so silly, joy is found,
With pie charts drawn in summer heat,
And snack breaks, oh, they can't be beat!

So here's to life, that wacky ride,
With hiccup laughs and brittle pride,
For when we chase those shadows sly,
We find ourselves and wave goodbye.

Beneath the Frozen Surface

Under ice, where penguins slide,
We wonder where all dreams reside,
With frosty breath, we poke and prod,
In search of meaning (or maybe cod).

Snowflakes whisper, 'Find the fun,'
As we pretend to be the sun,
With hot cocoa and silly hats,
Combing jokes like playful cats.

In snowball fights and snowy laughs,
We toss away our better halves,
To dance with shadows, twirl with glee,
And question if we're really free.

So raise a toast to frozen days,
And all the quirky, fun-filled ways,
For beneath the chill, we find the spark,
A warmth that glows within the dark.

When Paths Converge

We stroll through parks, lost and found,
Two clowns with balloons, quite profound.
Is it fate or just luck's delight?
A dance of socks in the moonlight.

Should we chase the sun or the next ice cream?
Life's a funny, topsy-turvy dream.
We stumble and laugh, take a silly bow,
Finding the meaning—oh, how and wow!

Juggling thoughts like a circus show,
Should we do a cartwheel or take it slow?
With popcorn wisdom, bits all around,
Life's a quest, can't be confound!

So let's giggle and hop, enjoy every twist,
In this wild ride, we simply exist!
It's not about answers, but scents of delight,
Together in mischief, everything feels right.

The Melody of Moments

A kazoo playing tunes, silly and bright,
The clock is a joker, oh what a sight!
Every tick is a wink, every tock a jest,
Life's a grand playlist, just enjoy the fest!

We whirl through our days like confetti in air,
Dancing on rooftops, without a care.
With hiccups and giggles, we sip on our tea,
What's the answer? Just let it be!

In whispers of laughter, the truth starts to show,
Passing the punchlines with every new glow.
Moments strung like pearls, silly and bright,
Let's chase the absurdity, hold on tight!

So sing with abandon, dance like a fool,
In this grand melody, we're all the fuel.
Who needs a map or a magical clue?
Life's playful melody is just being you!

Where Infinity Meets Finite

In a universe vast, where socks go to hide,
A shoe with a name is now quite a guide.
Stars in the sky sing, planets spin round,
Is this big puzzle where laughter is found?

A cupcake with sprinkles floats by in a dream,
It whispers of wonders, an icing-filled gleam.
If this is infinity, where's the stop sign?
A finite escape, oh isn't that fine?

We chase after rainbows, they tease like a muse,
Collecting the giggles, refusing to bruise.
In every odd moment, with chaos and glee,
We find we're the fun, not just the debris!

So let's ride the laughter down time's slippery trail,
With silly companions, we'll never fail.
In the dance of existence, we waltz and sway,
In every breath's laughter, let's boldly play!

Unveiling the Essence

A dandelion's wish blows, floating away,
"Is it me or the breeze?" it seems to say.
Life's a quirky riddle, quite snappy and quick,
A carrot in hand is the ultimate trick!

Under the sun, we juggle our flaws,
With splashes of color and great applause.
Pancakes on ceilings, we try not to stare,
In this wild little zoo, who really cares?

To nibble on nonsense, a slice of delight,
To twirl with the evening, till darkness turns light.
We weave the whole fabric with giggles and fun,
In endless confusion, we dance like we've won!

So toast to the quirky, the strange and absurd,
In this playful journey, life's laughter's the word.
With hearts full of chuckles, we smile in the haze,
Every moment's a gift wrapped in whimsical ways!

Navigating the Maze of Being

I took a left where I should've right,
Got lost in thoughts from day till night.
The cheese is gone, just like my drive,
Wait, what was I saying? Ah, I'll survive.

Chasing answers with quirky grace,
Dancing through time, a frantic race.
Frowning at maps that make no sense,
Maybe life's just a game of suspense.

With every choice, a twist or turn,
For wisdom, oh, how I yearn!
But laughter's the goal that keeps me whole,
'Cause life is just a silly stroll.

So here I stand with arms akimbo,
Trying to find the easy limbo.
In this wild maze, I must confess,
I'm more of a jester than a success.

The Echoing Heartbeat

My heart beats loud like a marching band,
With whispers of wonder at my command.
Echoing thoughts that bounce around,
Why can't I find solid ground?

Life's a riddle wrapped in a wig,
Dancing through doubts, I feel so big.
I ponder with poise, or so I think,
Then trip on my shoes and spill my drink.

So here I sit with my quirky charm,
Imagining dreams while dodging alarm.
Each heartbeat's a joke that life plays on me,
Trying to figure out, 'What should I be?'

Maybe a dancer or a wise old sage,
Or just a funny face stuck on this stage.
With every thump, I chuckle and cheer,
After all, what's purpose if not fun, my dear?

Stories Written in Stars

Gazing up at the cosmic show,
Wondering why time moves so slow.
Stars scribble tales in twinkly light,
But none of them bother to share insight.

Wishing on wishes that fall like dust,
In every spark, I place my trust.
But all I hear is cosmic giggles,
As I trip over universal wiggles.

Constellations twist, a grand charade,
Mapping my mind, a lovely parade.
With every blink, another plot twist,
Like who forgot to send me the list?

I dance with the shadows, chase the glow,
In this starry dance, I put on a show.
If life's a story that I must tell,
I'll write it in laughter; it suits me well.

Labyrinths of the Mind

With thoughts like mazes, I roam so free,
Is this a path or a memory?
Lost in yarns that I twirl and spin,
Maybe my brain's just a big grin.

There's a door marked 'Wisdom,' but where's the key?
I stood there pondering, sipping my tea.
As ideas scatter like leaves in a breeze,
I laugh as my logic drops to its knees.

Each question a riddle, a playful jive,
As I bob and weave, trying to thrive.
But all I find are quirky sights,
Like a cat wearing socks and taking flights.

So let's embrace this delightful mess,
Laugh at the tangles, who needs success?
In labyrinths deep, I'll dance and twirl,
For in this chaos, life's a funny whirl.

Beneath the Surface of Being

Why bother with the grand design,
When coffee's brewed, and snacks align?
We dance through days with silly grace,
Chasing dreams that leave no trace.

Life's a puzzle, missing pieces,
Where laughter grows and doubt decreases.
In every joke, a truth may gleam,
Like squirrels plotting their nutty scheme.

So let's confetti our concerns,
And serve up lessons that life returns.
We play our parts in cosmic jest,
Enjoy the chaos, and just be blessed.

With every laugh, we're filled with light,
As we embrace the silly plight.
For deep within, we tend to find,
Life's about the fun, intertwined.

The Search for Significance

I sought a meaning, oh so grand,
To understand this quirky land.
But every sign was upside-down,
And giggles masked the solemn frown.

The wisdom's hidden in the quirks,
In tickles and in silly works.
With every riddle's playful tease,
I found myself among the bees.

They hum a tune, a buzzing cheer,
Suggesting not to take life near.
With honey sweet and flowers bright,
We laugh till summer turns to night.

So let us quest with pranks in tow,
For answers wrapped in slapstick flow.
In jest, we'll stumble on the key,
For life is meant for a jolly spree.

Tracing Footprints in the Sand

I walked along the beach one day,
With hopes as light as feathers play.
The waves erased my every stride,
Like life's a joke we can't abide.

With footprints, laughter soon would fade,
As the tide came in with its parade.
I tried to map my thoughts with shells,
But found them lost in ocean swells.

The grains of sand laughed 'neath my feet,
Mocking my quest with rhythmic beat.
For what's the point, I muse with glee,
If every trail is washed by spree?

So let's build castles, grand but quick,
And not forget the tides will flick.
In sandy joys, we find our light,
And dance like crabs in pure delight.

The Heart's Silent Inquiry

In quiet moments, thoughts arise,
Like popcorn kernels turning pies.
I ponder deep, a thinker's curse,
While munching snacks, I try to verse.

Why are we here? I often muse,
Amidst the whirlwind of life's fuse.
Perhaps it's just to laugh and play,
And nap through half the sunny day.

With every ponder, I loudly snack,
A crunch or two and thoughts fall back.
So munch away and chill in breeze,
For questions fade with peanut cheese.

In every bite, a truth I find,
Life's simple joys are intertwined.
So here's to snacks, and giggles fine,
In this grand jest, we brightly shine.

Through the Veil of Uncertainty

Why is it we fumble, trip, and fall?
Stumbling through questions, we want to call.
If life's a riddle, what's the right key?
Maybe it's just to hop like a flea.

Some search for treasure, some seek a mate,
Others just wonder if they're on a date.
Between the laughs and the sighs we blend,
Finding that life's just a silly trend.

Are we all just puppets on strings of fate?
Dancing and prancing, oh what a state!
Chasing the sun or avoiding the rain,
Each little joy erases the pain.

In the end, could it be just a jest?
To lark and to love, oh, isn't that best?
So here's to the laughs and each wild surprise,
Life's one big circus beneath the blue skies.

The Dilemmas We Weave

Caught in a tangle, we spin and we twine,
Searching for meaning, like sipping fine wine.
Should we take risks or wish for a sign?
Maybe we're lost, but it's still divine.

With maps in our heads, we wander the maze,
Bumping through life in a daze of bright haze.
What's the right step? It's anyone's guess,
As long as there's pizza, we're still blessed.

Do we climb the ladder, or sit on the ground?
The weight of our thoughts can be quite profound.
But giggles and chortles help lighten the load,
While we juggle our dreams on this winding road.

From starry-eyed dreams to socks that don't match,
Each quirky twist adds a spark to our batch.
In this nonsense dance, we may soon uncover,
The truth's in the laughter we share with each other.

A Symphony of Seeking Souls

We march to the beat of a curious drum,
Hoping for answers, but feeling so numb.
In this concert of life, who's playing the flute?
Maybe it's the cat in a shiny new suit.

The questions we ask sound like notes in the air,
Dancing and twirling, with style and flair.
Is there a reason we chase after dreams?
Or just to mess up and hear the loud screams?

What if the magic is lost in the grind?
Like socks in the dryer, it shifts every kind.
As we croon to the moon and groove to the stars,
We might just find wisdom in giggles and scars.

So let's raise a toast to this sporadic quest,
Twirling and swirling, we'll give it our best.
In the symphony played by these seeking souls,
The laughter and chaos is how we find goals.

Fragments of a Fleeting Dream

In the blink of an eye, it all slips away,
Searching for magic in an ordinary day.
Are we just pixels on a grand screen?
Or actors with dreams that are rarely seen?

The clocks march on, like unending vines,
Plotting their course, while we sip on cheap wines.
With humor our sword, we battle the gray,
Filling our lives with jokes on display.

What if the secret is not in the plan?
But rather the crunch of a fresh cookie can.
Moments of laughter, small joys that delight,
Illuminating pathways in the darkest of night.

In the end, we're just stories poorly told,
Searching for meaning while we grow old.
So let's gather the fragments, make them our theme,
Laughter's the glue in this wacky dream.

The Fire Within

There once was a flame, quite daft,
It flickered and danced, a craft.
It wondered aloud, "What's my aim?"
Then tripped on a log, igniting its fame.

With s'mores and some jokes, it made quite a fuss,
"I may burn, but at least I brought us!
Life's a roast, let's laugh and ignite,
For popcorn's the prize on this wild flight."

Its glow turned to giggles of light,
As marshmallows toasted with all of their might.
"Who needs a goal when you can just glow?"
The fire just chuckled, "It's all in the show!"

Then out came the bugs, buzzing around,
As sparks turned to giggles, joy fully found.
In life's silly play, we might all prepare,
Just poke the kindling, humor's in air!

Embracing the Enigma

I asked a wise owl perched high,
"What's life for?" it blinked with a sigh.
With feathers all ruffled, it pondered some more,
Then hooted, "Just eat, sleep, and explore!"

The cat stretched and yawned, then joined in the fun,
"Chase strings, catch mice, or the warmth of the sun.
We're all just a puzzle, albeit a mess,
So why not embrace it, I must confess!"

A squirrel chimed in, with a twitch of its tail,
"Life's nuts, and my stash is not for sale!
Climb trees, gather acorns, and dash with crow's calls,
Or just watch the world from my lofty small halls."

So we laughed at the chaos, each story a gem,
In the tapestry woven, each thread was a whim.
"Who needs a map, when we've got our flair?"
Let's nibble on moments, forget if we care!

Seeds of Fulfillment

A seed in the dirt thought, "What's my plan?"
"I'm just chilling here, a mere little span.
Should I sprout? Should I squirm? Am I destined to grow?"
Then it heard the wind whisper, "Just take it slow!"

It decided to stretch and pushed through the soil,
With sunshine above, it had toiled.
"I'll grow into a flower, or maybe a tree,
Or just twist in the breeze, isn't that glee?"

The ants passed by, all busy and proud,
"Minding their business," they chirped, rather loud,
While the seed giggled, "Oh, I'm on a roll,
With all this fun, I could take on a stroll!"

So, bloom or just roam, it has yet to see,
With laughter around, what could it be?
In the garden of life, we all play our part,
It's not just the growing, but the joy in our heart!

Windows to the Soul

A mirror once laughed, "What's the scoop?"
"I reflect what you give, your expression, your swoop.
Life's quite the canvas, in colors so grand,
Splash on your laughter, make life really stand!"

A comic and joker waltzed past each day,
Turning each frown into a colorful fray.
"Why make it a puzzle? Just sprinkle some cheer,
Life's meant for the crazy, let's shift into gear!"

The window then chimed, "Peep over here!"
"The world's just a stage; let your heart steer.
You're faces and places, all swirling in glee,
So toss all your thoughts, let your fun spirit be!"

In the gallery of life, each jest is a place,
Where smiles are the frames in this wild, weird embrace.
So laugh with your eyes, let your spirit hold sway,
For joy's in the journey, come dance in the fray!

Canvas of Choices and Chances

On a canvas bright, we paint with glee,
Every stroke a choice, like sipping tea.
One day a clown, the next a sage,
Life's one big joke on a mismatched stage.

We juggle fate like it's a balloon,
Floating high, then bursting too soon.
Laughing at mishaps, we cheer and grin,
A dance of chaos, where does it begin?

Paint your worries with colors absurd,
In the gallery of life, be unperturbed.
Brush away troubles, let laughter flow,
The masterpiece waits for the next bright show.

With each twist and turn, we bend and sway,
Life's plot thickens in a comical way.
So, grab your palette, and dance while you can,
For when it all ends, not one will know when!

Embracing the Unknown

In the land of the weird, we step with dread,
Facing the fog, with our hearts full-fed.
Do we run in circles or dance in place?
With ducks in a line, let's embrace the race!

With mismatched socks, we leap and shout,
Whirling through life, avoiding the pout.
Sipping confusion from a crystal cup,
Do we go down, or just mix it up?

Like a cat in a box, we ponder and dream,
Is it all nonsense or part of the scheme?
Tickling fate with a poky stick,
Finding our way through the thick and the slick.

So let's hold hands in this silly ballet,
Twisting and turning, come what may.
With giggles and snorts, we'll embrace the ride,
In this circus of life, let's enjoy the slide!

The Journey Beyond Tomorrow

Tomorrow's a puzzle, with pieces to find,
A game of charades with fate intertwined.
As we hop on the train, tickets in hand,
Are we off to wonders or more shifting sand?

With binoculars on, we squint at the view,
What's coming next, is it pie or a stew?
Every twist and turn brings a chuckle or scream,
Are we sailing on rivers, or stuck in a dream?

The future is silly, with clowns on the way,
Making us giggle, come join in the play!
With confetti and laughter, we march along,
To the beat of the odd, we can't help but belong.

So hold tight your hat, let adventure begin,
We'll dance through the chaos, break out in a grin.
For the journey is wacky, mysterious, too,
And isn't that great? Just me and you!

Reflections in a Crystal Pool

In a crystal pool shimmering, we gaze and ponder,
Is it life's big riddle or just a wild wonder?
With ducks quacking loudly, and frogs casting spells,
We dip our toes in, where nonsense dwells!

What's reflected back? A wild-eyed grin,
The universe laughing, where do we begin?
Splashing around with the silliest fish,
Caught in the moment, fulfilled by a wish.

With ripples of laughter, we twirl and spin,
Catching glimpses of futures and places we've been.
Is it all crystal clear, or just a fun blur?
As life dances past, we giggle and stir.

So let's raise a toast to this wacky pool,
To shimmering dreams where we break every rule.
In reflections so charming, where laughter is bold,
We find our own stories, glittering gold!

Crossroads of Destiny

At this fork, I scratch my head,
Where should I go? Pink or red?
A hotdog stand calls my name loud,
But destiny's lost in the crowd.

Do I choose the left or right?
Both paths look silly at first sight.
I flip a coin and take a chance,
Hope this won't lead to a bad dance.

The universe laughs at my plight,
Sipping its coffee — what a sight!
I stumble on, still full of cheer,
My comedic journey, oh so clear.

In life's great play, I'm just a clown,
Wearing mismatched socks in this town.
With every choice, a laugh I find,
Each road I take, life's one big grind.

Ebb and Flow of Understanding

Like tides that rise and softly fall,
Understanding's just a funny sprawl.
I ponder deeply, then forget,
Is it wisdom gained, or just regret?

I read the signs like weird graffiti,
Each word is clueless, quite unpretty.
Do I grasp truth or just a lie?
My brain says 'yes', my heart says 'why?'

I trip on thoughts, fall flat on my face,
Life's weird puzzle, a hilarious chase.
With every mishap, I learn to giggle,
Searching for meaning, just a little jiggle.

In the end, I've made a friend,
In laughter's arms, I find the blend.
I flowing dance with joy so bright,
In this strange life, it feels just right.

Gazing at the Infinite

Staring up at stars so high,
Wondering if they all just lie.
Do constellations have a plan?
Or are they just dots on a span?

Is the universe one big joke?
With black holes where laughter's bespoke?
While I scribble down my grand dreams,
The cosmos chuckles, or so it seems.

Each galaxy swirls in cosmic funk,
While I munch snacks in my small bunk.
Am I here to discover or be found?
Or just eat chips while space spins round?

As I ponder the great vast blue,
Do any answers really come through?
With cosmic giggles all around,
I embrace this life without a sound.

Shadows of Tomorrow

Tomorrow's shadows play a prank,
Dancing light hearts, they burst and sank.
What will come? A pie or a mess?
Life's unknowns, just a fun guess.

I chase sunlight, it runs away,
While shadows giggle, "Never stay!"
Do I race to find what's ahead?
Or lounge on grass, wish dreams instead?

In this game of hide and seek,
Futures hide, but laughs peak.
Will I be wise or fail in flair?
Life's odd riddle — who really cares?

With every step, I trip and laugh,
In this chaotic, silly path.
In shadows cast and glimmers bright,
I frolic forth, embracing the light.

www.ingramcontent.com/pod-product-compliance
Lightning Source LLC
Chambersburg PA
CBHW072143200426
43209CB00051B/332